The Way Back Home

Title: The Way Back Home. Poems
© Nanne Nyander 2023.
www.nannenyander.se
Published by: BoD – Books on Demand, Stockholm, Sweden
Printed by: BoD – Books on Demand, Norderstedt, Germany
Cover, book design and drawing by Nanne Nyander.
ISBN: 978-91-8057-316-0

Do you want to come home?

A tribute to I.

1.

I'm staring desperately at the sky,
I'm howling at the moon, I curse the ocean.
This is not the play I was asked to be in.
Or is it?

2.

What would happen to the sky
if the sky thought it was a cloud?

3.

I'm going nowhere to find me.
I've been going somewhere for so long
and I'm still at the same place.
So why not surrender, raise the white flag,
and lay down my weapons?
I'm here, going nowhere.
I have finally arrived.

4.

Hold my hand, I need to get out before it's too late.
I'm going under before my very eyes,
and I don't even see it.

5.

I'm not what you think I am,
I'm not what I think I am,
I'm nothing,
and so are you.

6.

The days are going by,
while I'm trying to find my way back,
away from the illusion,
an illusion created by the mind.
Everything I see
throws me back into a story in my head.
I close my eyes,
but everything I hear reminds me of something,
and yet again, I'm back in the mind's territory.
"Focus!"
I am.
What am I?
A scent suddenly reminds me of my childhood,
and I'm back in the mind.
I am here, nothing else exists.
Feelings come over me,
is it fear?
Analyse, back in my head again.
When will this stop?
I am here.
I am.

7.

I want to come home,
home where I belong.
"You are already home,
but to be home is to know home.
Don't get lost in the quicksand of life."
I'm getting desperate.
desperate to wake up in your arms,
to finally be able to rest,
rest from this tiresome quest.
The quest to find nothing.

8.

I can touch you,
just by touching the air you breathe.
I am the air you breathe.
When will you see me for what you are?
We are one, we are everything,
we are nothing.
We are one.

9.

I have been looking for home my whole life,
like a lost seagull.
Who would have thought,
I was a turtle,
I have been carrying home with me the whole time.

10.

How can thinking be so sticky?
I can't move without getting entangled
in the web of thought.
No matter which way I turn,
it's there, my mind is not letting me go.
I am not a thought, I am not a feeling.
I want to wake up
from this persisting obsession with thoughts.
I know that there's no one here to wake up,
so what am I searching for?
The absent seeker,
that thinks it is controlled by thoughts?
Thoughts that are not even real,
just some passing clouds
on a perfectly clear sky.

11.

I can fly,
teach me to walk,
walk on this planet,
without bumping into everyone's hidden secret.
Teach me to be,
be without losing myself.
I feel everyone's pain, I feel everyone's lies,
I feel everything.
Let me be whole and one with you,
with everything, with nothing.
Let me be nothing.
I am lost without me.
Lost enough to wake up,
wake up to the truth that I am.
I am.

12.

So silent, says the mind.
Go beyond the silence the mind creates.
Let it be silent without the word silent.

13.

My mind is luring me
into the imaginary world of thinking.
Into the veil that distorts everything.
The gravitational pull is overpowering
and I'm moving towards thought like a magnet,
I can feel the gravitation getting weaker and weaker.
But the pull is an illusion,
imaginary pictures floating around in space.
I'm here.

14.

Save me from my mind.
Guide me back again and again to my pure being.
Life is like walking on a slack-line,
till it's not.
Life just is.

15.

I'm sitting here, watching my mind,
as it is throwing up millions of things as bait
for me to take.
I know the game now,
I can see how the rules are made to alter,
every time I think I know them.
I can't think my way out,
I can't outsmart the mind with another thought.
I'm here, I watch the mind and its tricks.
I leave it alone,
it will sooner or later lose its interest in me,
and I, in it.
I'm here,
I'm here watching the mind,
I'm here.

16.

When was I me?
Have I ever been me?
Was I me before I was born?
It's time to wake up from this sleepwalking identity.
It's time to live as the one I am.
It's time to live.

17.

Can you see my light?

18.

Wonderful me, created out of nothing by no one.
Because I am nothing, and so are you.

19.

Leave everything behind,
rest in the silence that you are.
I will catch you when you fall,
when you fall in love with the silence within.

20.

Solitude,
running into the forest of the mind,
holding on to my lifeline to feel anchored in the I.
I run,
I run around in circles,
not knowing how to stop,
I'm calm,
I'm focused,
I am still.
Nothing is moving.
Everything is vibrating.
Emotions get thrown out into open space,
colliding with all the contents of the mind.
Leave me not,
pull me in,
I'm way too confused to carry on.
Everything stops.
I'm here,
it's silent, am I dead?
Or have I found my way back,
back to the place that I never left?

21.

I feel like something wants to come out,
something is stuck inside of me.
How do I let it out,
how do I let go?
Back in the mind again.
Feel,
let go.
How to let go of holding on?

22.

Go within and solve the non-existing problem.
I'm ripped into pieces,
my heart is crying out in pain.
What to do in this insane world
where no one is listening?
Go within and find peace.
The silence is leading you to wake up.
No time to sleepwalk.
No time.
Wake up!

23.

Thoughts, no thoughts.
It makes no difference.
Sing your thoughts to the universe,
till the thinker can stand no more.
Sing as if your life depended on it.

24.

I am moving out.
Should I send you a card with my new address?
I'm moving away from familiar ground.
I have stayed here long enough,
it's time to move.
I'm moving out.
I will have so much more space,
I'm moving.
I'm moving out of my mind.

25.

Who am I?
I touch the sky with an open hand,
welcoming me to rest in the movement of stillness.
The soul is the one on the journey to liberation.
Can I return home now?
I open my arms and let you rest with me.
We can lie here in the hammock of consciousness,
watching the world go by.
I hold you in my arms,
letting you rest with the knowledge that we're home.
Here we are one,
here we can watch the world go by.

26.

Barefoot I run through the war in my mind,
barefoot I run through the meadows.
What is real?
Am I here,
or am I stuck in the mind's creation?
I need to get out.
Barefoot I run on broken glass.
I'm hurt, but I still keep running.

27.

In the movie in my head,
I'm not acting anymore,
I have left the scene.
I am now content with just watching.
How did I ever get dragged into this movie?
I can see it, it's still going on,
but I'm not interested anymore.
I'm watching,
I interact,
but I'm not stuck there.
I'm the one,
I'm the one watching,
I am one.

28.

Breathe, breathe,
how can such a beautiful world be so cruel?

29.

Being lost in the basement of my mind,
looking for the missing pieces.
Every time I'm getting air beneath my wings,
ready to fly out of the attic,
my mind finds half a missing piece,
and sends me back into the basement to find the rest.
Is it just another trick of the mind,
not wanting me to wake up?
It's hard to ignore,
the need for resolution is so very strong.
But my determination to wake up is stronger.
I stay on guard,
I stay vigilant,
preparing to soar into the empty sky once again.

30.

Soul on the run to nowhere.
Catch me when I fall.
I leave myself on the ground
and continue on my own.

31.

What am I,
if not a sign that everything is ok?
What am I, if nothing is real?
What am I, when the world has gone to pieces,
what am I?
I'm everything, I'm nothing,
I'm the good and the bad.
What am I, when nothing is left to fight for,
what am I?
I am one,
I am one as everything,
I'm nothing.
I am.

32.

War in the mind of the one that is broken,
broken into tiny pieces.
With the fire in my heart,
I will melt it all together,
and once again, we will
be one,
one whole,
one.

33.

Am I here to find the truth,
or is the truth here to find me,
or are we one and the same?

34.

Remember who you are.
Everything is veiled by the interpretation of the mind,
but I am strong,
I am strong enough to see through it.
Still, the mind sucks me in when I least expect it.
I feel totally helpless,
but I AM strong enough to resist.
I just have to find the strength,
I know it's here somewhere,
Why is it hiding from me
when I need it the most?

35.

Sailing through the night sky,
looking for you.
Are you still dreaming,
or are you awake,
awake to reality,
awake to the truth?
Sail with me, through the sky,
till we reach the end of time.
We are going nowhere,
and it's a beautiful journey.

36.

Was it I, who walked this path before,
or was it someone else?
In my mind there is no one,
no one will search for awakening anymore.
Do you think no one will find it?
I'm no one, I'm nothing,
I'm everything.

37.

Wandering in the dark looking for the light.
Why not go to the light and search there?

38.

My mind is still lurking in the background,
trying to make an entrance,
feeling it is so very important.
It's just a funny play to watch.
The mind can't fool me anymore.
It's like the chatter from distant people in a cafe.
But I decide what I want to focus on,
I focus on whatever I want,
without believing it's me.

39.

I'm looking for the one, that's looking for the one.
What are you looking for?

40.

When is now the right moment to wake up?
I ask myself, but who will answer?
I'm not there anymore,
I'm here watching the show.
It's always now.
Now is always the right moment to wake up,
and now, and now.

41.

All I can think of is you.
When will I be reunited with my true love?
There is no when, there is no then,
there is only now.
See, feel, don't think.
No thought can take me there,
no amount of thinking can take me there.
Thought keeps the distance visible between me
and my beloved.

42.

Silence will take me there.
There is nothing but silence,
noise can't interrupt the silence,
and neither can thoughts.
No matter how loud my mind is,
there is still silence.

43.

I can feel the pain of the planet.
I can feel the PAIN!
How can this be?
An empath trapped in a human body.
You think we're moving forward,
but we're standing still,
creating so much pain.
Let me go.
If it wasn't for the pain,
I would not need to be here.
If it wasn't for love,
I would not be here.
I'm one with the planet,
I'm one with everything.
Hurt me no more.
We're all one.

44.

To see is to look without your eyes.

45.

I'm making tiny pictures,
on a canvas that is bigger than anyone
can ever imagine.
My tiny pictures seem to get lost in the divine,
chaotic masterpiece,
but still, the masterpiece wouldn't be whole
without me and my tiny pictures.

46.

Walking around with our heads in the sand,
dust in our eyes, not being able to see.
Life is not what we think it is.
Like the river flowing, you are the river,
jump into yourself and just be.
The silence is here,
listen closely and you can hear it behind all the noise.
Feel it.
Let there be stars underneath my feet.
Let there be rain pouring from my eyes.
Let there be summer in my heart,
melting the winter away.
There is only I.

47.

Knock, gently knock, knock me out flat.
I knock on heaven's door till I'm blue,
but no one hears me.
I see, I feel, too much.
Is it time to wake up?
My time is now!
Time does not exist.
I AM awake!

48.

Let me go, my life has gone past me
when I was looking the other way.

49.

Watch me walk away from this dream
where most beings are sleepwalking.

50.

I walk alone,
trying to stay hidden from the enticing mind.
Thoughts are my distraction from I.
This is it.
Now, not later,
only now exists.
My brilliant mind has fooled me all my life.
Later is its game.
"Later, later, later.
What about tomorrow?
Then, then you will work twice as hard."
Save me!
I know, I know, I know I can see it.
Help me to overcome my weakness to distraction.

51.

Find the peace inside your heart.
Find your way home.

52.

The backpack is getting too heavy to carry.
Let me take it off, and never pick it up again.
Let me be free, free of the heavy load I carry,
in my conviction that it is me,
that it is life.

53.

My soul is taking me home.

54.

When will this end, my friend?
When will I see the light?
Who or what can I trust?
Not the mind, not the body, only I.
I walk alone and that is the only way I know.
I walk alone, till I reach the end,
and then,
I walk alone.
Because,
there *is* only I,
and
I walk alone.

55.

No one can make me move away from myself,
not even my mind.

56.

I'm not my body, I'm watching my body move.
I'm not my feelings, my feelings come and go.
I'm aware, now I'm feeling sad,
it's just a feeling.
Now I'm feeling good, it's still a feeling.
I'm meditating and feeling that I'm getting closer.
Closer to what?
It's a feeling and a thought.
I'm not my thoughts, pleasant or unpleasant.
It's a thought and a feeling,
a feeling and a thought.
I can watch my thoughts
making these feelings come up.
I can watch my feelings
making thoughts stick to them.
A thought is a thought, a feeling is a feeling.
I'm neither.
I'm not my memories.
Memories can be true or not true,
they can be altered, modified or
blocked out altogether.
I'm not my beliefs.
My beliefs can change from one day to another.
My beliefs can be absolutely bonkers.
My beliefs can make my ego feel good.
I'm not my ego.

I'm the space where it all exists.
I'm the space where beliefs can come and go.
I'm the space where my mind can judge my beliefs,
and then add another belief to that,
about judging,
or a belief that I'm a good person,
because I have this belief.
But I'm neither,
I'm the space where all this is happening.
I'm the silent watcher.
I am nothing,
and,
I am everything.

57.

Mind is holding me in a tight grip,
wanting me to stay.
Mind is fine with being bored,
desperate, confused, fed up.
It likes being the one who is sad and depressed.
This is not what I want,
but the mind doesn't mind.
I want to be free and happy.
Mind doesn't mind either way.

58.

I push myself till I no longer can push,
I'm no longer the one that pushes and strives,
I'm not even the one that gets pushed.
I'm the one that watches it all.

59.

The child I once was,
wished for an off button to switch her mind off.
pondering over,
who would turn it on again?
I still haven't found an off button,
but I'm getting closer,
closer to accepting there is none.
I just have to turn away and stop listening to the mind.
Can it be that easy,
and still so difficult?

60.

Words, words, words.
Some words have wings,
they fly straight into your heart,
and wake you up.
Some words can kill,
but it's not the owner of the words
that decides in the end.
It's the receiver.

61.

Am I avoiding life, or is life avoiding me?

62.

Don't be afraid. I've got you.
You can let go and be what you truly are.
What you are, behind all the masks that you've created,
created to cover your face,
to disguise who you truly are.
Just let go,
I've got you.

63.

Into magic-land, I disappear, when I'm not vigilant.
Into magic-land, I lose myself completely.
Into magic-land, I disappear,
and get lost in the magic of the mind's creation.

64.

Who am I?

65.

If I could only,
if I could only stay still.
*"Why are you moving around,
like a hungry sparrow chasing a butterfly?
Stop chasing!
You don't want to catch it, you want to be it."*
One day I will turn into a butterfly.
But ONE DAY is the obstacle,
one day will never come.
I AM.
*"Stop chasing,
just be."*
If I could only,
if I could only,
be still.
If I could only,
just be.

66.

Farewell, my friend,
I'm here holding your hand, but I'm leaving.
I'm going home.
I have overstayed my visit a long time ago.
Now it's time to let go,
time to move on, or not move at all.
You're the one moving, moving away from me.
I'm here, I'm still. I'm not moving.
I'm here holding your hand saying goodbye,
as I see you vanish around the corner.
You're still holding on to me,
or am I holding on to you?
It's time to let go.
It's time to go.

67.

Sing to me,
you sing the most beautiful song I have ever heard,
sing to me, sing once again my beautiful soul.

68.

One step forward, two steps back.
Two steps forward, one step back.
Why are you moving at all?
You're already here.

69.

I'm stuck in my own illusion,
my illusion of not getting anywhere.
I'm moving forward,
but I'm standing still.
I need to let go,
let go of everything that is holding me back.
I have to let go of my thoughts of being stuck.
I need to move on,
I need to finish what I have started.
There is no going back.

70.

Life is holding me down on the ground,
when all I want to do is fly,
spread my wings and just soar over this beautiful,
distorted landscape.
But I'm here on the ground, playing in the mud,
looking for home.
Looking for home has been my mission.
I now know where home is,
but the final step seems impossible.
I'm stuck in the mud of my own creation,
or is it, *my* creation?
The more I struggle the more I'm stuck,
sinking deeper into oblivion.
My only comfort is that I have seen home,
I felt it,
I know it's here.
I know where I'm going.
Like a lotus flower, I will emerge from the mud.
I'm going home.

71.

I am a tiny cloud in the clear blue sky.
I am the sky that lets the cloud move freely.
I am the one looking up at the sky in amazement.
I am the one.
I am one.

72.

Fragmented memories,
lost or not lost are holding me back.
But aren't they just memories?
What am I?
Not a memory.
Small tiny memories not quite remembered,
are keeping me bound to this world.
Why do they come up now?
I was so near, everything was so calm.
Everything was so clear.
And now I'm up in the mind again,
trying to find solutions to the non-existing problem.
The jigsaw puzzle doesn't want to be solved,
doesn't want to be put together,
doesn't want to reveal the whole picture.
But does it really matter?

73.

Stop moving, stop grasping,
stay where you are my friend.
I'm here.
If you leave yourself alone, if you just let go,
I will be here to catch you.
I will hold you in my arms and love you forever.
Nothing can keep us apart.
You and I are one.

74.

I stumbled into life without a map or a compass.
What was I thinking?

75.

Mind is an illusionist,
making up an unbelievable world out of nothing.
The illusion is so believable,
I can't take my attention away from it,
it's got me totally hooked.
This illusion is not a child's game,
one can really get hurt.

76.

Sleep no more,
wake up beside me and sense the feeling of being
home.

77.

If I had thought all my life that I was a mountain,
would I be convinced that it was so?
I have believed that I was a somebody,
somebody separate from everything else,
a somebody who's in pain.
My whole life I have believed in this story.
What if it isn't true?

78.

Mind is a magician creating the most convincing
illusions.

79.

How could I travel away from here,
when here is always with me?
Here is always here,
no need to move away,
here is everywhere,
no end, no beginning,
here is all there is.

80.

When is the best time to be here and now?

81.

Thoughts moving around in space,
who do they belong to?
Some of them used to be mine,
at least that's what I thought,
they don't stay long enough for me to claim them.
One minute they are here, the next they're gone.

82.

Is this it?
Am I home?
Mind is doing its thing, but I am still here.
I'm still home.
Is this it?

83.

How is it that I'm still here wandering around,
thinking I'm lost, going nowhere?
I think too much.
Or is that even me?
My focus is on the silence I perceive inside,
but my mind is too enticing,
and me is still too gullible,
easily distracted into the mind again.
Let me go now!
I'm here,
I can see the thoughts,
I can even see the thought, "I'm here",
appearing in front of me.
I can see it all,
but still, it keeps getting stuck to me like velcro.
This sentence is flowing in front of me too,
like a boat on the drift.
It all appears in empty space,
without my doing.
No need to grab hold of every thought
that comes my way.
I'm here watching it all,
watching it all passing by.

84.

Don't be afraid of letting go.
I've got you.

85.

Who was the one who got me here in the first place,
was it me or was it me? It's only me, it's only one.
I must have planned this on my own,
I am responsible for this journey's outcome,
and so are you,
because you are me and I am you,
we are one.

86.

I'm moving too fast, mind can't keep up.
But I'm not moving.

87.

I can feel the pull of the mind.
Why can't I ignore everything, and just be?
Be free, stop running to the mind,
every time it snaps its fingers.
Will I ever be free?
I'm here!
I know I'm here!
I'm so lost,
but what's so lost?
What am I?
Be my anchor,
I don't want to drift away.
I keep getting sucked up by the mind,
into a world that doesn't exist.
I'm aware!
I'm aware of getting lost.
Something has to be aware of the lostness.
What am I?
I'm aware, I'm awareness.
No, I'm lost.
Who knows that I'm lost?
The lostness, the confusion,
the non-ability to focus, are so vivid, so solid.
But none of those are me,
I'm the one being aware of all of it.
I'm the one watching this boring movie.
It's the most dragged-out scene that ever existed.

The audience has left, and so should I.
But I can't find the exit.
Back again to being lost,
still watching, being bored, still watching.
I'm here inside somewhere,
or am I outside?
I've always been on the outside looking in,
but now I'm spread everywhere and nowhere.
I've always been lost in this world,
maybe it's because
I believed that I was inside this body,
looking out.
But I'm not inside this body.
I'm free.
I am.
I'm everything and nothing,
I'm the bird in the sky.
I'm nobody.
I'm the perfect example of me.
Let me soar in the sky,
till I lose sight of the lost human being,
on the ground,
trying to be found.

88.

Silence is here prior to everything,
with or without noise.
I am here prior to everything,
with or without thoughts or emotions.
I am silence.

89.

Being without you, my beloved,
is profoundly loud and lonely.

90.

I'm resting but not resting,
I have landed in the empty space,
I'm one with the empty, silent space,
it's what I am.
I'm empty,
everything that shows up is just a movie on the screen,
the screen of consciousness.
I'm getting smaller,
at the same time as I'm getting bigger.
I am the empty space and I have no borders.
Be vigilant.
The big things,
the loud thoughts, are easy to detect.
What about the small things I still think are me?
I can see, they are not me at all,
they are just small thoughts
that used to slip through the cracks.
I'm vigilant.
I can now see them come and go,
without underestimating them.
Sometimes they are so small that I take them for
what is me,
but they are not me,
they do not belong to me.
I'm empty space, and the space is empty.

91.

We slumber by the fire of life
when dawn comes upon us.
Stranger there, speak to me, how did we become two?

92.

I live under the radar of the mind.
I live where equilibrium exists.
I'm silence.
Fasten your lifeline here
before you get dragged into the next story.
Be equipped for excursions into a world of illusions.

93.

Don't leave me behind.
I know it's all in my mind.
Take my hand,
take me with you.

94.

Clouded head of mine,
waiting for the storm to come in and clear the sky of
thoughts.

95.

The illusion is like a labyrinth,
and I've found my way out.
I never was in it,
I have always been here.
The labyrinth was only in my head.

96.

I'm here waiting for no one,
I'm here not waiting, I'm here waiting for me.
When will I stop running around looking for myself,
and finally find me?
I'm here waiting and watching.
When will I find myself?
I'm here completely visible, but I don't see me.
Why am I running around?
If I only slow down I might see me.
I might realise that I've always been here.
I'm not just an image in the mind,
an image that I believe is me.
If I only stop running,
I might see
that I'm already here.

97.

I'm staying in the land in-between.
In between me and I.
I'm moving back and forth,
thinking I'm something.
It's time to let go,
it's time to let it all drop away.
I live in the land in-between.
It's so easy to get lost here.
I lose my sense of direction,
but I am determined to succeed this time.
I have been here before.
The longing for home is getting unbearable,
the longing for home moves me forward,
the longing for home is my everything,
till I finally accept,
that I AM home.

98.

I'm on my way to nowhere,
to become nothing.

99.

Stay with me,
give me strength to carry on,
or maybe that's the problem.
I always find the strength to carry on,
but what if I didn't?
What if I just let go?
Maybe my perseverance is the problem.
It's time to let go,
it's time to stop struggling.
I'm here,
I'm silence,
I'm nothing,
I'm everything.
What can possibly be wrong?
Wake up!
I can still see the struggle,
but, struggle, or no struggle,
makes no difference.
I AM HERE.

100.

Mind is trying to delay me finding myself,
mind is playing hide and seek.

101.

How can I continue on this journey,
without a compass showing me the way?
You are my compass.
Am I moving towards liberation,
or am I moving towards destruction?
I move, but I don't move.
I'm here waiting but not waiting.
I'm ready.
I am already,
I am awake.
I know I'm awake.
Help me to overcome my doubt.

102.

Snowstorm outside, but inside it's calm.
I can't be touched by the storms anymore.
I'm here watching it in wonder,
seeing the beauty of it all.
Isn't it magnificent?

103.

See, be, watch the world go by.
You are already home.

104.

I'm leaving all thoughts,
all thoughts about a better future,
a future where I will be enlightened.
I'm leaving all thoughts,
all thoughts about the past that do not exist,
it's just in my mind, played up again and again.
Memories are visiting me to keep me occupied.
Mind does everything to keep me stuck in illusion,
but I'm here.
I can see the thoughts, they are not me,
they are just being presented to me,
to see, or not to see.
I choose not to go there.
Who's the I, who chooses or doesn't choose?
It is all just happening without my control.
I'm just here watching,
I am here.

105.

What am I?
Nothing is holding together anymore.
Or is nothing holding everything together?
Am I nothing?

106.

Stars in the sky,
reflecting on the ground I walk on,
if I stretch out my hand I can touch them,
I'm home.
The journey to nowhere has been so long.
Still, no time has passed.
Now is all there is,
and now is now,
and now,
and NOW.

107.

I have a mission,
and I'm going to make it.
My mission is very important.
My mission is to live.

108.

Breathe, breathe,
how can such a cruel world be so beautiful?

109.

The wanderer is waking up,
the journey has come to a stop.
No more searching,
the wanderer has woken up.
She woke up in my arms and now we are one.

110.

Look on one side of the veil and you can see me.
Look on the other side and I'm gone.

111.

Grateful am I, to be alive.
Alive for the first time.
Grateful am I,
to be awake.

This is the end, my friend.